An Investigative Look Into StoneCrest Behavioral
Hospital

By Daniel K. Arnold

Disclaimer:

The perspectives shared in this publication are from the point of view of one journalist and the people he interviews.

Names have been removed for privacy and will only be revealed to select agencies for safety reasons when the information is available.

Remember there are multiple sides to every story. This document is one investigative journalist's attempt to be honest.

An Investigative Look Into StoneCrest Behavioral Hospital

By Daniel Arnold

About The Journalist:

I have been a resident of Greater Lansing my entire life. I love Jesus and following God is my top priority.

I have a special interest in the safety of others and advocating for the broken. I have a degree in Elementary Education from MSU and completed the LCC Honors Program.

I currently serve on 2 consumer advisory councils involving the rights of mental health consumers. I have written 10 books and 3 online publications.

I have written this investigative publication after spending time on the highest security wing of

StoneCrest Behavioral Hospital as a patient in
Detroit.

I want everyone to know that they have a voice
and that Jesus loves them.

You may contact me for advocacy and assistance
at:

voiceoftheunheardlansing@gmail.com

Inside StoneCrest Chapter 1

By Daniel Arnold

I am here to talk today about looking at StoneCrest
Behavioral Hospital as objectively as possible. I
have been hospitalized twice on the first floor of
StoneCrest that has an all male and all female side.
I was not in the best mindset and I received
injections twice the first visit.

They seemed a little vigilant at the time:
"Step away from the nurses' station. I said, "Step
away from the nurses' station. All right, get the
needle."

Chemical restraint followed by disorientation is
inhumane to me. I believe in minimal levels of
restraint with supervision to help patients settle
down.

The 2nd time I came to StoneCrest they seemed much more kind. I think this was because I just needed a med switch. I was in a better frame of mind.

Today I write you from the point of view of a patient admitted a third time to StoneCrest-- this time completely against my will.

The police rang my doorbell close to midnight and I woke up. Three officers showed up and asked me if I was on drugs.

Hello! I was asleep!

I was taken to CMHA-CEI Crisis Services, then Sparrow Main, then StoneCrest. I had no access to court records of why I was committed until I ended up in StoneCrest Crisis Wing on the 4th Floor.

When I was supposed to have intake I said, Hi my name is Daniel Arnold. I am an investigative journalist. If there is any corruption in your hospital, I will report it to L.A.R.A. (MI Licensing and Regulatory Affairs).

I was surprised. Everyone seemed so chill and nice except for one person. Maybe I was receiving preferential treatment for announcing myself as an investigative journalist.

However, God allowed me to record on paper aspects of this hospital that few know. Let's see what we can do to make this world a better place!

Inside StoneCrest Chapter 2

Patient #1:

This story is captured to show a perspective. See what you can gather from the details of this interview:

"Okay, last month was horrible. They make me want to sue them possibly. They assaulted me. First 3 hours to Provident Hospital first for back problems a month ago.

Forced me to come to hospital-- petitioned. Attacked me over a deodorant top. 20 people put me on all fours. Me not fighting back, just moving in position. Same type of techniques 3 times. 3rd time started to fight back with little punches and kicks."

We look at this case study to find out what it's like to be a mental health patient who doesn't trust staff around him. It's a complex situation and happens in the blink of an eye.

It must be stressful to work in a mental hospital and it must be stressful to be a patient. The more we can understand eachother the better.

(Interview Continued...)

Daniel A:

How can things improve here?

Patient #1:

Better interviews. Doctors should talk to patients more.

Daniel A:

What do you want to talk to the doctors about?

Patient #1:

Medication. Discharge of the time.

Daniel A:

What do you want the doctors to discuss with you regarding medicine?

Patient #1:

Types of meds, name, how many. Should give us side effects sheets automatically explain it more further before shot. Just give shot instead of explaining it like a human being.

Daniel A:

The Psychiatric Team will benefit by taking more time to answer every patients' questions as best as possible. This is what I gather from this interview. Let's dig a little deeper before we come to a conclusion.

Inside StoneCrest Chapter 3

By Daniel Arnold

Daniel A:

What do you like to do for fun?

Patient #2:

Family, Friends, Workplace and file representing

through breeches of administration.

Daniel A:

If you could do any job, what would it be?

Patient #2:

Biomedical, Technical, Engineering Services

Daniel A:

What kind of education do you have?

Patient #2:

Pharmacy, 8-10 years of medical school

Daniel A:

What is most important in this world?

Patient #2:

My family, God

Daniel A:

I like to dig in and see the beauty in Mental Health

Consumers. It was great to hear this patient open

up.

Inside StoneCrest Chapter 4

Case Study From Crisis Wing:

Patient #3 claims to be the Lord Jesus Christ,

mentions the word "kilo" and talks about making

money from cocaine.

Patient #3 mentions wanting to shoot the president.

Patient #3 says to me, "Donald Duck is going to

bite your ___ off. You talk too much."

Patient #3 says, "All we do is sell cocaine."

"They're going to chop up your body and

everything."

Patient #3 says to staff, "I'm not a private

investigator; I'm a mercenary."

Alone these statements seem isolated, but together

they point to a person that needs supervision.

If you want to receive a copy of the compilation of my investigative research, you may e-mail me @ voiceoftheunheardlansing@gmail.com

Inside StoneCrest Chapter 5

Patient #4:

Announces that he is Agnostic and God told him: "Humans don't have to eat animals. Think of the chickens."

Patient #4 says, Hospital staff say they support every religious view.

Patient #4 mentions "nuts and seeds instead of meat. They don't have the choice."

Patient #4 said he asked the hospital for vegetables.

Daniel A:

It is awesome to see consumers stand for what they believe in no matter what situation they are in.

Patient #4 is an example of a consumer that may be misunderstood.

I understand his feelings and am learning to be a

better advocate every day.

Inside StoneCrest Chapter 6- Advocacy

There are many different ways to raise awareness

for ourselves and others. When I moved to the 4th

Floor Restorations South from the Crisis Wing I

met a woman who needed a little advice about her

meds that were not working right.

I felt her pain and remembered what it was like to

be doped up on the wrong meds. I told her to wait

and see if the meds worked. Then, communicate

with the whole medical team-- to discuss about

getting a med switch if necessary.

She was very thankful.

Inside StoneCrest Chapter 7 - Advocacy Part 2

I noticed another female patient struggling in front of the Med Nurses Station. She claimed she was having an allergic reaction. No one knew what to do including me.

The nurse told her to step away and get the help of another nurse. The patient buried her head in her hands and sobbed.

All I could do was tell her I would listen.

Sometimes that's all we can do.

Inside StoneCrest Chapter 8 – Time At
Restorations

Everything is peaceful. One guy is raving in front
of everyone saying things like "Paid in Full." It
agitates people some, but most are patient with
him.

This man begins raving in front of the TV Room.
A confrontation starts up with another man. I
stepped in and talked him down. He left the room.

"A gentle answer turns away wrath (Holy Bible)."

Always follow-up with consumers personally to
understand the depths of a situation that led to
escalation. Try to get past the stress of the
moment.

Inside StoneCrest Chapter 9 – Spirituality

Amazing, Supernatural is our God. I love to see consumers get excited about God's Word.

Many people have asked to borrow my Bible and I am delighted as long as they read it in the same room as me. I am so blessed to see others like me get blessed. "We are in this together."

Inside StoneCrest Chapter 10 – Patient #5 and #6

Patient #5:

Age: 48 year old male

Daniel A:

What are your hobbies?

Patient #5:

Work and stuff

Daniel A:

What is important to you?

Patient #5:

Thinking about myself sometimes.

Patient #6:

Age: 58 year old male

Daniel A: Why are you here?

Patient #6:

Because I am hiding out here from people that are trying to kill me. I have been threatened 4 or 5 times in the last month.

Daniel A:

Do you trust the staff?

Patient #6:

F___ no.

Daniel A:

Why do you feel that way?

Patient #6:

I was asked to do sexual acts which I did not.

Daniel A:

Who asked you?

Patient #6:

(Patient #7) on a day to day basis. He says I'm his wife.

Daniel A:

Have you reported him?

Patient #6:

Yes. They shot him up last night.

Daniel A:

What do you do for fun?

Patient #6:

I play music. I'm a song writer. Retired Ford employee.

Daniel A:

Have you ever filled a Recipient Rights Complaint?

Patient #6:

I don't know what one is, so no.

(I taught him.)

Inside StoneCrest Chapter 11 – Recipient Rights Complaints

It is difficult for the average consumer to fill out a complaint. They must be brave enough to walk up to the box, get a pencil, and share their story.

Many times their communications are disoriented and illegible. Today there were no forms available and we had to request forms.

(The first time I requested forms at the front desk of StoneCrest Floor #1 years ago they asked me why. This was very unprofessional as the process must be discreet.)

Inside StoneCrest Chapter 12 – Boundaries

I noticed at StoneCrest Behavioral Hospital they have a no touch policy.

Usually I break this technicality but I believe staff in particular need to follow it.

About ten minutes ago a staff member fondly touched the bottom of my foot (sock part). This is not okay. I don't appreciate staff personally trying to dominate so I politely corrected him.

At Behavioral Health Center of Michigan a staff person who seemed nice randomly touched the shirt part over my belly. When I told another staff member about it, she talked what a good person he is.

There is no excuse. Use physical boundaries with consumers.

Inside StoneCrest Chapter 13 – Hospital Bulletin Boards

It is a necessity that mental hospitals be clear in the patient bulletin white boards. At StoneCrest 4th Floor Restorations South, it seems the chart goes un-updated.

This is a serious matter because patients do not have technology to verify the date. They have to trust in a white board with incorrect information.

Inside StoneCrest Chapter 14 – The "Little" Things

Note On The Door:

I walked into my room, but it was closed. When I opened the door, an unknown voice said, Hello. It was maintenance workers with a ladder. Courtesy would have been to put a note on the door to alert me and the staff. This is unprofessional.

Sensitive Documents:

2 patients have left documents with potentially sensitive information on the table. The best decision is to look for the owner of the document if you know them. If you don't, send the document to the front desk.

Coffee Time:

People like a nice Cup O' Joe. It is comforting and reminds consumers of home. The staff at StoneCrest frequently put out cups filled with coffee for everyone on the unit. This is thoughtful.

Spiritual Advocacy:

More than once, I have seen staff eager to hand consumers Bibles. One time a staff overheard a consumer asking me for a Bible. I told him he could read mine in the same room as me, but before I left the hallway the staff attentively placed a Bible in his hand.

On another occasion, a different consumer requested a Bible, but the first two staff only had a New Testament for him. As he walked away, a third staff member delightfully pulled out a full Bible to give to him.

Trash:

The trash is full in the day and there is a lot of vegetables on the floor in the phone room. The hallway bathroom has on the floor too. Janitorial response to patient notification of the mess was good.

Hospital Bracelets:

Are med nurses required to scan bracelets?

They don't.

A staff member mistakenly reminded me that I am probably leaving today. She was thinking of another patient.

Cussing Staff Member #1:

Staff to Consumer:

"Don't say no s___ to me like that Mother_____."

(3/09/19, 6:00am, In front of Room #30, Crisis Wing.)

I didn't hear anything else. The staff member was being loud.

Same Patient to Front Desk:

"Scuse me b___. What time is the food coming?

(Patient has filed Recipient Rights Complaint and so have I.)

Cussing Staff Member #2:

"I want them to start scrapping so they can knuckle

his a__ up."

Inside StoneCrest Chapter 15 – Discharge

One painful aspect of staying at StoneCrest Behavioral Hospital is the usage of the word "discharge."

A frustrated consumer who is already going through mental anguish can become even more distressed when they are led to believe that they will be going home soon.

Yesterday, a social worker mentioned "discharge" to me as I said, but meant it for another person.

Today my psychiatrist said, "Keep doing what you are doing. You will be leaving in a few days."

If I am doing things right, than why am I being held here?

The StoneCrest Team needs improvement in the discharge process. They need to communicate with each other better and be very clear when talking to consumers about discharge.

Inside StoneCrest – Chapter 16 – Female Patient Perspective

Patient #8:

Everyone in here has never done a damn thing to me since I've been in here."

Daniel A:

What's it like here?

Patient #8:

It's fine. Food's good. People are nice. You gotta stay. You gotta stay. The workers are f___ mean. They steal. They steal everything they can from you. White Pine was the worst, maybe Hurst.

Daniel A:

Why was White Pine the worst?

Patient #8:

They stole everything they could steal from you.

They dump out your purse. I'm ___ pissed.

Inside StoneCrest Chapter 17 – Conclusion

As this investigative journey into StoneCrest Behavioral Hospital comes to a close I wonder what I have missed as an individual.

How can I look at the positive?

Many staff greet me with a smile and share how they are doing. They are humans and deserve to be treated with the same dignity as fellow patients. It has to be hard for the janitorial department to clean urine off the floor. Being a security guard stuck in the elevator must be difficult as well.

Who can I believe? People here are in crisis and not always honest. I can only take down their stories and report on what I see.

"God help the outcasts—Children of God

(Disney's The Hunchback of Notre Dame)."

Addendum #1:

I did not intend to write more, but I am very annoyed. A staff person woke me up at 5:30am. I experience night terrors every night. If vitals are necessary at this hour, the staff could've been polite without rudely rushing me.

Addendum #2:

The activity therapist played my song selection for the group:

Evanescence: Wake Me Up

This is a good cultural exchange in Detroit.

Addendum #3:

It's wrong for the group therapist to talk in great detail about a patient to make a point about boundaries. Staff should not corporately talk about a patient and use him/her as a case study.

Addendum #4:

I heard a young lady saying that like 10 guy patients in the hospital have asked her to suck their

_____.

This is despicable. What kind of world do we live in? Women need a safe place.

Made in the USA
Middletown, DE
01 February 2025

70275736R00026